Get a free coloring book
and more at
heroesoftheword.com

Illustrated by Dream Computers
& Visage Art Productions

Design by Jonathan Sparks
Edited by Jonathan Sparks
Published in 2023
First Published in Canada by Visage Art Publishing
Owned by Visage Art Productions
Richmond British Columbia, Canada

Library and Archives of Canada (LAC) Act
Data is available upon request

ISBN 978-1-7389945-2-6
heroesoftheword.com

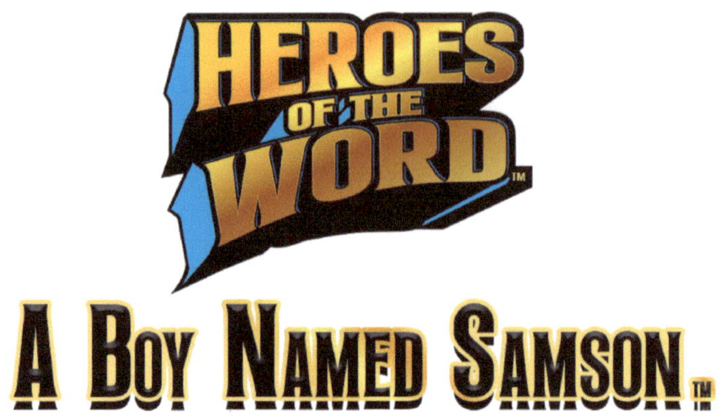

A Boy Named Samson™

By: Jonathan Sparks

Discover the incredible story of Samson in Judges 13-16.

**Out in the
field one day,
a woman knelt down
and began to pray.**

She asked God to
give her a baby boy.
This simple request
would give her so much joy.

God sent His angel
to give the good news
that she would have a son
that would lead the Hebrews.

The boy named Samson
grew up big and strong.
His beard grew thick
and his hair grew long.

No one could match
his strength, you see.
Not man, nor beast,
they all had to flee.

A thousand Philistines
were no match for him.
With a donkey's jaw,
they took it on the chin.

God blessed Samson
and made him a judge.
The Philistines didn't like him,
and they held a grudge.

They tried to find a way
to make Samson weak.
So they paid Delilah
to convince him to speak.

Samson, tell me
how you became
so big and strong?
He told Delilah
it's because
I let my hair grow long.

God blessed me with strength
because I trust and obey.
But if I cut my hair,
my strength will go away.

Delilah waited for Samson
to fall asleep,
then she cut his hair
like a little shorn sheep.

God left Samson because
he broke his vow.
So the Philistines made Samson
work like a cow.

They chained him to
a giant millstone.
Where Samson would spend
his life all alone.

Blind and humiliated,
Samson had his fill.
He prayed to the Lord
for forgiveness
and to do God's will.

God took pity on Samson
and returned his strength again.
Samson pushed down the walls
and left the Philistines slain.

For you see, God loved Samson
and He loves you too.
He wants to give you strength
so you will always come through.